HAMSTER CARE GUIDE

The Complete Hamster Care Guide. Everything You Need To Know About Hamster, Housing, Feeding, Choosing And Taking Proper Care Of Them

MARK JASON

Table of Contents

CHAPTER ONE

INTRODUCTION

Hamsters can look like a cute and cuddly choice whilst you are searching out the proper puppy, however how lots do you simply recognize about hamster care, and how need to you put together to welcome a hamster into your private home.

In this guide to hamster care, I give you the essential information you need to get commenced as a hamster owner!

CHAPTER TWO

CHOOSING THE PROPER TYPE OF HAMSTER

The maximum common form of hamster that human beings have as a puppy is the Syrian hamster, which is also regularly referred to as the Golden hamster. This little rodent initially comes from the northern regions of Syria, and the south of Turkey. It's miles taken into consideration to be inclined as a wild species as its habitat is underneath danger from destruction through human beings. There may be no such hazard to Syrian hamsters in captivity.

Some other famous kind of pet hamster is the dwarf hamster. There are 3 sorts of dwarf hamsters which might be related, and that you'll generally see in pet shops, the Roborovski, and the two forms of Russian dwarf hamster, iciness White and Campbell's. The fourth kind of dwarf hamster is the Chinese language; this is not associated with the other kinds of dwarf hamster.

Just like humans, one-of-a-kind hamsters are appropriate to unique situations and homes. So the primary selection you need to make is what sort of hamster you need, and that's nice appropriate to you and your instances.

Syrian Hamsters

Determine what type of hamster you want, and then choose the proper home for them!

The first thing to recollect about Syrian hamsters is that they have to constantly be kept with the aid of themselves; they're very territorial and will fight with different hamsters.

Syrian hamsters are the biggest of the captive hamster breeds and they are often the most popular as pets. They have a active character and may be virtually fun to watch and have interaction with. If you take care of them from an early age Syrian hamsters may be trained nicely, when you have bit patience. They may be commonly slower pace than dwarf hamsters so they are easier to preserve up with, particularly at some stage in the education procedure.

The common lifespan for a Syrian hamster is two to 2.five years, even though like maximum animals, there are some people who live longer than this.

As a person the average size of a Syrian hamster is 5.5 inches. Syrian hamsters are popular with beginner hamster owners, and younger children, as they have a tendency to be simpler to handle and tame.

Dwarf Hamsters

Dwarf hamsters are, because the name shows, smaller than Syrian hamsters. They can usually be saved in a cage with other dwarf hamsters however you still need to test for any symptoms of upset or aggression, at which factor they may need to be separated.

The Roborovski dwarf hamster is the smallest of the dwarf hamsters, and doesn't develop a lot more than three inches in period, even as an person. Roborovski dwarf hamsters are very speedy and lively; they have got frequently been recognized to run as far as one hundred miles in keeping with night on their hamster wheel. Those lovable little creatures stay for a median of three to 3.5 years.

Russian dwarf, iciness White hamsters get their name from

their ability to turn white in the wintry weather months of their wild Russian habitat. In captivity they commonly hold their darkish gray coloring due to the presence of synthetic warmness and lights. In addition to dark grey you can also see winter White dwarf hamsters with different coloring, inclusive of marbled, sapphire, pearl and sapphire pearl. These lovely little rodents have an average captive lifespan of between 1.5 and a pair of years.

Campbell's dwarf hamsters are the dwarf hamsters which might be most customarily found in pet shops. Inside the wild they're located in China, Russia and in different areas of critical Asia. Their dark grey look may be very much like that of the iciness White, and that they have a comparable lifespan; averaging round 2 years.

Chinese language dwarf hamsters are in reality extra correctly named honestly Chinese language hamsters, however they're regularly wrong for a dwarf hamster due to their small stature and the dorsal stripe that they have got in commonplace with wintry weather White and Campbell's dwarf hamsters.

They've a mean lifespan of 1.5 and a couple of years.

THINGS TO CONSIDER BEFORE GETTING A HAMSTER

Don't forget these pointers whilst shopping for your hamster!

Once which sort of hamster you need there are some matters which you want to keep in mind while you visit the store to pick out your new puppy.

1. Try to move later inside the day

Hamsters are livelier inside the nighttime than they may be in the course of the day. That is whilst you are maximum probable to see the real character of a hamster. If you go to a pet shop too early inside the day it's in all likelihood that the hamsters could be slumbering. You aren't going to be able to tell if the one you are looking at is just performing as everyday for a hamster, or is usually a touch lazier than maximum.

2. Ask to take a more in-depth appearance

In case you ask the puppy save proprietor to show you a hamster near up this may do two matters. It's going to display you the way the hamster reacts to being treated, and it's going to allow you to peer in case your destiny pet looks healthful. You must in no way purchase a hamster that has a moist tail, bald spots or lumps (besides for the scent glands on their legs). You must also make certain that the hamster you purchase has easy ears and a smooth, dry bottom. Manifestly there's usually the danger that your pet becomes unwell at some point after you're taking them home but you at the least need to make sure they are healthy after they go away the store.

3. Watch the way the hamster acts

When the store proprietor handles the hamster you are hoping to buy then you'll be in a position to check out its temperament. Preferably you need to pick out a hamster that is energetic and inquisitive, and appears to be pleasant. You don't really need to buy a hamster this is very frightened, and also you sincerely don't need a puppy that's competitive!

4. Have a look at the environment

A first rate deal of a hamster's health and circumstance can rely upon the environment in which it is stored. It's now not normally an awesome concept to buy a hamster that has been saved in cramped, grimy or damp situations.

5. Ask about the age of the hamster

From the age of approximately 8 weeks girl hamsters can be pregnant so that you need to try to establish the age and sex of the hamster you're looking to buy. Hamsters are quality purchased on the age of 4-6 weeks as they're simpler to tame if you take care of them from approximately that age.

6. in no way be afraid to ask questions

Maximum puppy shop proprietors could be happy to provide as tons information as they can approximately a hamster, so don't be afraid to ask whatever you want to know. In case you simply stand there and receive the primary hamster you're offered then you are not likely to get the puppy you really want.

CHAPTER FOUR

PREPARING A HOME FOR YOUR HAMSTER

Don't overlook that you couldn't purchase a hamster without also shopping for a suitable home to your new bushy friend to live in.

If you make a decision which you select Syrian hamsters then you are, of course, going to have to shop for a bigger cage than you will for a dwarf hamster. However there are other factors to don't forget too; you need to offer a top notch deal of notion to exactly what sort of domestic is excellent for the new addition in your circle of relatives.

The significance of cage length

Selecting the proper cage is important to a hamster's fitness and properly-being

Hamsters want to have lots of area to run round; and that doesn't mean loads of pipes, it manner real ground area.

consistent with the country wide Hamster Council, a Syrian hamster need to preferably have a cage that has floor area of as a minimum 1000cm2   and a top of 19cm.

A dwarf hamster needs to have at least 750cm2 of ground space and a cage top of 17cm.

You must continually ensure that the ground of the cage has a overlaying of at least 4cm depth of suitable bedding as hamsters like to burrow.

It's crucial to word that it's no longer an excellent concept to buy cedar or pine shavings on your pet as some hamsters can develop a hypersensitivity which causes problems with their breathing.

Cord and plastic cages are both famous varieties of housing for hamsters, and they each have their advantages and drawbacks.

In case you choose a twine cage then your new puppy gained't is short of somewhere to climb; and this is something that hamsters like to do. One factor you need to make certain of is that the wires are in no way greater than half a centimeter aside as it can be dangerous if they may be any wider aside; a hamster can end up inquisitive and get stuck, especially a dwarf hamster. You have to also by no means buy a cage that has a twine backside, as this is not excellent for a hamster's toes.

If making a decision on a twine cage, make sure to apply layers interior, in order that in case your hamster is hiking along the top of the cage, they don't have too some distance to fall in the event that they lose their grip. This stops your puppy from hurting themselves. It's espccially important to have regard to this when your hamster is a baby as they could get severely harm in the event that they fall from an excessive stage.

There are many plastic moulded hamster cages available on the market these days. Those hamster homes are very easy to easy, and that they provide safety to your little buddy, when you have other pets in your own home. Many of those cages have a small vicinity of cord that could act as a mountain climbing frame on your hamster. if you purchase a cage that doesn't have someplace for you hamster to climb, you need to make sure that you provide a mountain climbing body in the cage for them so they're unfastened to climb whenever they want to.

One very essential factor to keep in mind about a hamster cage is that it needs to be get away evidence. You would be amazed at how adept these cute looking creatures can be at creating a bid for freedom!

Ensure that there aren't any gaps your puppy can squeeze through, and constantly take a look at that doorways are completely comfy. If they are in any way unfastened there is a great danger that your creative little hamster can be able to open them.

The importance of toys

One very vital thing which you need to bear in mind, while you're setting up a home to your hamster, is toys. Hamsters love to have something to preserve them occupied; a wheel on its personal isn't sufficient.

In addition to the same old hamster wheel you need to offer a ramification of other toys, which includes timber chunk toys. These toys are an exceptional choice as they provide a fun interest to your hamster whilst, on the equal time, stopping their teeth from turning into overgrown.

You want to ensure which you only supply your pet wooden this is secure, and no longer dealt with pesticides. Cardboard is likewise a favorite with hamsters. You could get pet pleasant cardboard rolls from stores if you are involved about the glue and ink which can be found in commonplace family cardboard gadgets.

One very important object in a hamster's cage is someplace for them to cover away; like a in particular made hamster house. Your puppy will need a place to get away to, specifically for sunlight hours snoozing, so you want to provide this for them. A phrase of warning, with any plastic items for your hamster's cage you want to keep an eye fixed to your puppy's interaction with the item. In case your hamster begins to bite and swallow the plastic that is awful for them.

Getting ball for your hamster

One of the essential toys that a number of people buy after they first get a hamster is a hamster ball. most people have likely visible the brightly colored plastic orbs careering round a person's ground, run best on hamster electricity.

Maximum hamsters will fortuitously use a hamster ball, even though you have to never force your puppy to achieve this if they seem reluctant. We'll take a look at the use of a hamster ball in greater element whilst we keep in mind the exercising your new hamster will need. Suffice to mention that maximum of these cuddly rodents will enjoy tearing around your home in a ball, so it's in all likelihood an awesome idea to encompass one for your shopping listing.

FOOD TO FEED YOUR HAMSTER

in case your hamster become living in its herbal surroundings it might be consuming seeds and grasses, plus a few insects. Hamsters are clearly omnivorous, simply as people are. The herbal hamster meals that you could buy at the puppy keep is made to imitate the seeds and grains that a hamster could devour in the wild. You must choose this herbal food, rather than the fairly colored varieties which may additionally appearance exciting, however which frequently incorporate a whole lot of components.

as soon as per week you can recollect giving your hamster an fit for human consumption treat through imparting some meal worms, or a small amount of boiled egg. Those are favorites with maximum hamsters, and they're also wealthy in protein so that they make a first rate addition in your pet's diet.

Continually understand that you ought to never deliver your puppy whatever sticky to consume. if you do it may get caught in their cheek pouches and purpose an injury.

Providing fruits and veggies for your hamster

Your hamster will like to eat fruit and veggies, but you should be careful not to provide them too much. A small dice of fruit or vegetable, two or three times a week, is extra than enough.

Be very cautious while giving your hamster carrots to eat. Your furry pal will really love them, however it's important to keep in mind that carrots are complete of herbal sugars and should be supplied as a deal with, not as part of a hamster's regular weight loss program.

Other culmination and greens that your hamster will like consist of cauliflower, broccoli, pear, peach and banana. Constantly do not forget to dispose of any uneaten meals from your hamster's cage so that it doesn't rot.

One of the essential troubles is that a hamster will frequently beg for food even if they're not hungry. They keep the behavior that they've in the wild, and save food of their cheek pouches to consume later. Within the wild that is because hamsters look for meals at night, which they then take returned to their underground home.

This doesn't suggest that they sleep all day within the wild; they do in reality awaken and snack at the cuisine that they have got amassed. In captivity is essential for hamsters to build up a large inventory of meals as they constantly have access to fresh nourishment in their cage. So, they will continually beg for extra to stash away, however most effective feed your puppy as a whole lot as they want to devour.

The PDSA recommends that a Syrian hamster needs to be fed approximately 10g of dry meals twice a day. It may marvel you to examine that a dwarf hamster needs about the identical. They will be smaller in stature but they have a higher metabolism than Syrian hamsters.

Best time to feed your hamster

Many humans assume that hamsters don't devour at all for the duration of the day however as we've already cited this isn't genuine. Hamsters surely doze for the duration of the day but they will nonetheless wake to devour at times, so there's no damage in imparting a touch food inside the morning and a little inside the nighttime.

The principle issue is to ensure your bushy accomplice has the proper quantity of meals, and that clean meals is furnished at each feeding time. The water on your hamster's water bottle must additionally be changed each day, and the bottle needs to be washed very well at least as soon as per week.

Type of water to give hamster

Many people supply their puppy hamster water straight from the tap, but water high in chlorine is not desirable in your pet. It is mostly an accurate idea to present your hamster filtered water to drink in case you live in a place where the faucet water contains a number of chlorine, or other chemical compounds.

CHAPTER SIX

GETTING CLOSE TO YOUR HAMSTER

When you have bought a hamster from a pet keep you then is probable going to have to spend a while mastering your new buddy so that they turn out to be tame and trusting. After the primary 24 hours has elapsed you can begin the method.

It's vital to word that you could need a variety of staying power, turning the new arrival right into a ball of fur that sits luckily in your hand does not typically take place in a single day. Hamsters all have their very own person personality, and they all take specific quantities of time to become tame enough to address; the system might also take weeks or even months.

The fine way to begin coming near your new pet is as a bringer of treats. Reflect inconsideration on it, it's natural to accept as true with someone that treats you nicely, and brings good matters to eat. Positioned a treat at the palm of your hand and placed your hand within the cage, for the hamster to method. You should do this inside the night whilst the hamster is maximum energetic. By no means disturb your bushy friend when they are asleep and in no way positioned your hand in their personal vicinity; the distance inside the cage in which they can hide away, or the house you have bought them. In case you try and pressure your hamster, encroach on their territory or disturb their shut eye then you definitely are by no means going to earn their consider.

After a few days you could start to pet your hamster when you give the treat; this could assist to develop a pleasant bond. After a similarly few days you could attempt scooping your hamster up with both palms underneath them; don't attempt selecting them up together with your hand. in the event that they look uncomfortable, or they try to chunk then place them gently back down and deliver them a treat. You need to always do that near the ground, or any other secure surface, in order that if you do drop your hamster they will not get harm.

After you've finished this sometimes your new buddy have to start to stroll onto your arms robotically and you can start to have a few actual bonding times along with your puppy.

Remember that you need to by no means disturb a hamster whilst they're snoozing and that you should in no way make loud noises around your new housemate. Hamsters can be very nervous of unexpected and loud sounds so that they can be very satisfied with you in case you are being noisy around them.

As soon as your hamster is accustomed to their new domestic, and you've began to bond with them, you want to make sure that the tiny rodent is getting sufficient exercising. if you have sold the right length cage, so there is lots of ground area on your hamster to run around, then this can hold your puppy somewhat occupied; as will the wheel within the cage that is constantly a fave.

Further you ought to try to make certain that your hamster gets some time outside of the cage in a hamster ball.

CHAPTER SEVEN

CHOOSING THE RIGHT HAMSTER WHEEL

With a wheel, your hamster can run highly long distances without ever having to depart domestic. In reality, hamsters walking in wheels have been recognized to run greater than five miles in a single night time!

All this strolling is amazing workout for your hamster, because of this they're more likely to stay in shape and healthy and no longer get too fat!

Both steel and plastic hamster wheels are available and every kind has its very own pros and cons

Steel wheels are possibly to remaining longer than plastic wheels. However, steel wheels are usually made with rungs in preference to as one solid piece (like a ladder and like the wheel pictured inside the caricature above). Sadly, hamster legs are pretty fragile and might effortlessly get injured if they fall thru the gaps between rungs even as walking.

Plastic wheels are regularly made from one strong piece of plastic – in preference to rungs – that is safer for the hamster, as there aren't any gaps for his or her legs to fall via.

Hamsters normally prefer larger wheels. The larger a wheel is, the much less the hamster has to arch it's again and the extra comparable it's far to jogging on flat floor inside the wild.

Going for walks with an arched back is very terrible for a hamster's fitness. In case you ever see your hamster arching their again whilst strolling then you should purchase a bigger wheel for them as quickly as viable.

We suggest a wheel length of 12 inches for Syrian hamsters and 8 inches for dwarf hamsters.

CHAPTER EIGHT

HEALTH CARE ISSUES OF HAMSTER

As soon as you have got a puppy then it's your obligation to make certain that they're taken care of; especially whilst they're ill. Obviously you don't want this to take place, however there is always the likelihood that your hamster turns into ill in some unspecified time in the future.

It is able to every so often be tough to tell if something is incorrect together with your hamster. Inside the wild hamsters are preys for large animals, so they are attempting not to reveal if they're harm or feeling unwell, because it makes them inclined.

If you get to understand your pet well then you may possibly have a sense if something isn't always as it ought to be. There are a few signs and symptoms which are well worth looking out for.

• Lack of urge for food

• Smaller poop pellets, or none in any respect

• Sitting nonetheless and not using a motion in any respect

- Eyes no longer vibrant and alert whilst wide awake

- Unknown discharge across the nostril or eyes

- Aggression when now not typically competitive

- Bald patches

- Exchange in actions

- Damp tail vicinity

- Alternate in posture such as hunching

- Trade in respiration

- Limb chewing

- Alternate to ingesting habits

In case you be aware any of those adjustments on your hamster then you definitely have to seek recommendation from a vet.

One very last factor with reference to fitness: If your property could be very cold for some cause, and your hamster seems to be subconscious, then it's worth placing the cage somewhere heat to see if the exchange has any impact. Hamsters can move into hibernation if it's bloodless and you may find that's what has happened. If this is the case then your hamster need to awaken as soon as they may be in a warm environment.

THE END